EGGS

by **Marilyn Singer**

illustrated by

Emma Stevenson

Holiday House / New York

To Darling Starling and friends
M. S.

For my Mom, Dad, Richard,
Rachael, Lorrainne, and
Megan-Louise
E. S.

Text copyright © 2008 by Marilyn Singer
Illustrations copyright © 2008 by Emma Stevenson
All Rights Reserved
Printed and Bound in China
The text typeface is Mrs. Eaves.
The artwork was created with layers of gouache
on 300 gram hot press watercolor paper.
www.holidayhouse.com
First Edition
1 3 5 7 9 10 8 6 4 2

Library of Congress Cataloging-in-Publication Data
Singer, Marilyn.
Eggs / by Marilyn Singer ; illustrated by Emma Stevenson.— 1st
ed.
p. cm.
Summary: Explains the varieties, functions, and characteristics
of the eggs of a multitude of creatures, including insects, birds,
and reptiles.
Includes bibliographical references (p. 30).
ISBN 0-8234-1727-1
1. Embryology—Juvenile literature. 2. Eggs—Juvenile literature.
[1. Embryology. 2. Eggs.] I. Stevenson, Emma, ill. II. Title.
QL956.5 .S56 2003
591.4'68—dc21
2002017117
ISBN-13: 978-0-8234-1727-8

IT'S A QUIET CRIB.
It's a bobbing boat.
It's a private pond.
It's a room with no view.
It's walls to break through.
It's breakfast, lunch, and dinner.
It's an egg.

Every type of animal in the world needs to make more of its own kind. Dogs, cats, elephants, whales, bats, and most other *mammals*, including people, give birth to live babies. So do garter snakes, great white sharks, scorpions, and other animals. But many animals, including all birds and spiders, most insects, fish, and *amphibians*, and even a few mammals, lay eggs instead.

It usually takes a male and a female to make babies. Females make the eggs. Males *fertilize* them with *sperm*. When birds, *reptiles*, mammals, insects, and some amphibians mate, the eggs are fertilized inside the female. Then she lays them. Other amphibians and fish *spawn*, which means that most female fish and amphibians lay their eggs first and then the male sheds sperm over them to fertilize the eggs.

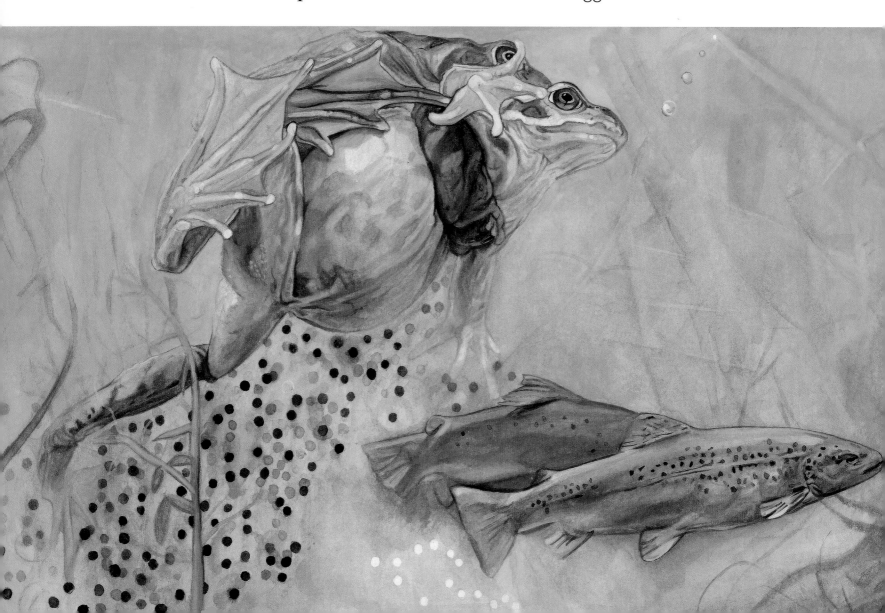

Each egg is a special world. Inside an egg, an *embryo*—a developing baby—can get food and drink, breathe, and grow. The food and drink are in the *yolk*. Each embryo starts as a dot on the yolk. The yolk will give the baby enough food and liquid until it is ready to leave the egg.

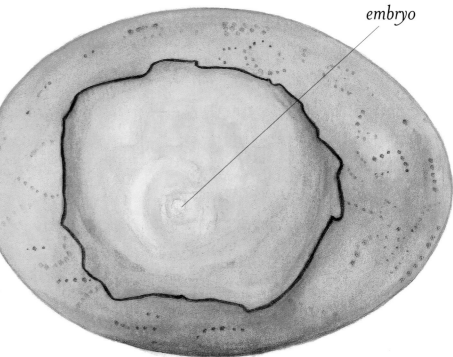

embryo

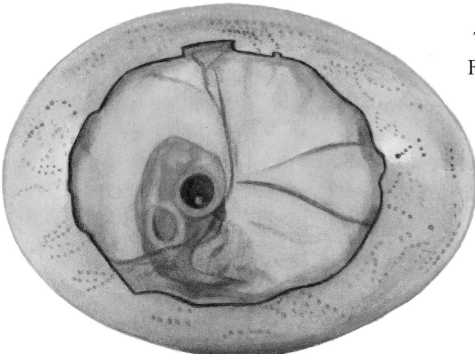

The embryo needs oxygen to breathe. Fish, amphibian, and some insect eggs can take oxygen right out of the water. Land eggs get oxygen from the air. The oxygen passes to the embryo through the egg's covering. Eggs with shells have tiny holes to let in new air and let out old.

But for an embryo to survive, its egg needs more than a yolk and oxygen. Each egg must be at the right temperature so that it doesn't freeze or overheat. That is one reason many animals choose warm spring days to lay eggs. Many insects and spiders are exceptions. Their eggs have a thick, watertight outer layer to survive winter weather. The egg must also stay moist. Land eggs are already moist inside their shells. Eggs without shells need to be in water so they don't dry out. Water also acts as a cushion to protect the embryo from bumps and bruises in its soft egg.

An egg may feel squishy, firm, or hard. Fish and amphibian eggs are soft. Reptiles and birds have eggs with shells. Inside the mother, the yolk gets coated with egg white, or *albumen,* and covered with a shell made mostly of the mineral calcium.

Soft fish eggs have a thick skin around them. Some kinds have a drop or two of oil inside to help them float through the sea.

Reptile eggshells are hard, leathery, or papery.

Like other amphibian eggs, a bullfrog's are covered with clear jelly. When the jelly touches water, it swells and helps the egg rise to the surface of a pond.

Bird eggshells are always hard, but their texture varies.

Duck eggs feel soapy.

Tinamou eggs are as slick and shiny as china.

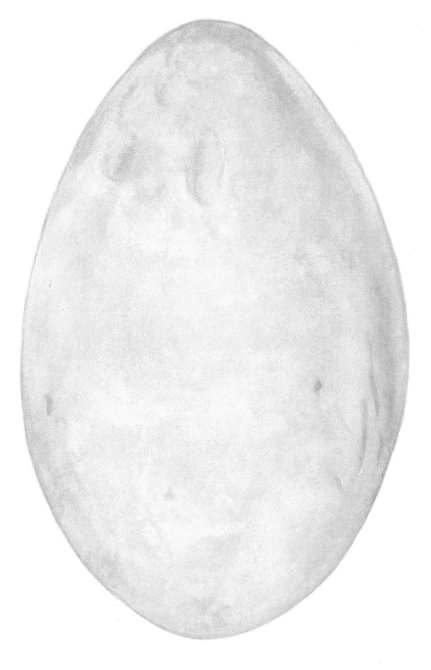

Flamingo eggs are powdery.

Whether hard or soft, eggs come in many sizes.

An insect called a Trichogramma wasp lays eggs too small for us to see inside the eggs of several kinds of moths and flies.

An ostrich lays eggs so large each could hold one pint of liquid or nineteen chicken eggs. But an ostrich egg is nowhere as big as the egg of the enormous and extinct elephant bird, which lived in Madagascar three hundred years ago. It was large enough to contain two gallons of liquid or more than one hundred hen's eggs!

Eggs come in many forms, too.

Insect eggs can be round, oval, long and slender, flat as a disk, or some other shape. They may have ridges, grooves, ribs, or pits.

We think of birds' eggs as "egg-shaped." This oval form gives eggs strength so they won't break when the parent birds sit on them. But birds' eggs vary somewhat in shape.

A murre's eggs are more like cones, with wide bottoms and narrow points. That shape lets them roll in a circle so they won't fall off cliff ledges where they're laid.

A sea turtle's eggs, which are buried in the sand, are as round as Ping-Pong balls.

An owl's eggs are nearly round.

An octopus's eggs look like grains of rice glued together in strings. They hang beneath sea ledges or in underwater caves.

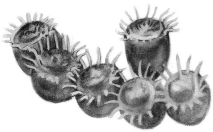

The stinkbug's eggs have crowns of spines, probably to bring in air.

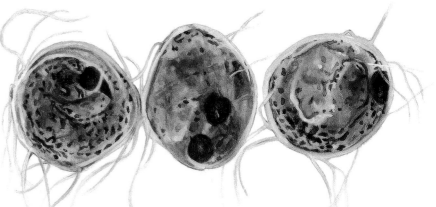

A flying fish's eggs have long threads to catch on to seaweed so they won't float into dangerous waters.

Eggs come not only in different forms but in all colors—not just chicken-egg white or brown.

Round, pearl-like salmon eggs are orange.

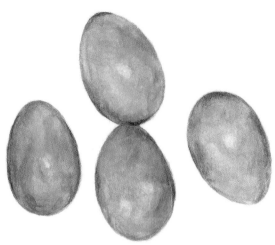

Hard-shelled robin eggs are blue.

Sturgeon eggs come in shades of black, gray, and golden yellow. These are the fish eggs we call caviar and eat in fancy restaurants. Salmon roe is sometimes called "red caviar." People eat these orange eggs as well.

The eggs in a *clutch*—a single group—are usually all the same color. But some animals' eggs vary a lot.

Common murres' eggs have the widest variety of colors and patterns of any bird. They may be deep blue-green, bright red, brownish yellow, pale blue, cream, or other shades, with spots, blotches, lines, or no patterns at all. Why do the murres' eggs differ so much? The birds nest in great colonies on cliffs. Parent murres can tell which eggs are theirs by their distinct appearance.

Some eggs are not distinct at all. They are *camouflaged*. They blend in with the background so that *predators*—hunters—can't find them.

Many butterflies and other insects lay green eggs on green leaves. These eggs are hard to see.

Terns and skimmers nest on beaches; these birds' eggs often have patterns that resemble the sand or stones.

Burrowing owls and other birds that nest in burrows and tree holes don't need camouflage. They usually lay bright white eggs so the parent birds can see them more easily in the dark.

Every species produces a different number of eggs. Most birds lay a fixed number of eggs each season. Some will lay more if theirs are removed or destroyed. Chickens and ducks have been specially bred by people to keep laying so that we can have fresh eggs to eat daily. One chicken set a record by laying 361 eggs in 364 days.

In places free of danger, animals don't have to produce a lot of eggs, but in the oceans where many predators lurk and where eggs can be swept away into treacherous waters, fish and other animals lay millions of eggs. Scientists once counted nine million eggs in a seventeen-pound turbot, a type of fish. Only one in a million is likely to grow into an adult turbot. Some dragonflies that shed eggs into rivers and ponds full of hungry fish and frogs lay thousands of them.

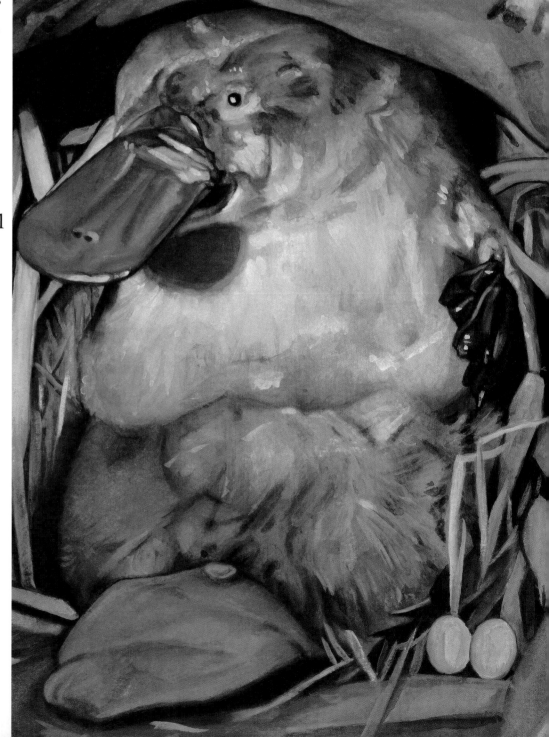

The giant albatross, a seabird, lays one egg every other year on far-off islands that have few predators.

The platypus, a mammal that lives in Australian rivers, lays two soft-shelled eggs in a snug burrow on the bank.

Many wasps, bees, ants, and termites
live in colonies—or groups. They need
workers and guards to care for the eggs,
the *larvae*—babies—and the nest. Most
colonies have a single queen, whose job is
to lay lots and lots of eggs to hatch into
workers and guards. A termite queen
lives for fifty to one hundred years. In
her lifetime, she may lay as many
as a billion eggs.

Eggs have a long list of enemies—wasps, snakes, skunks, mites, baboons, crows, vultures, fish, and people, among them. Laying a huge number of eggs is one way to make sure some of them will survive. Another way is to lay poisonous ones. The cane toad, the longnose gar fish, and the rattlebox moth are just a few of the species which lay eggs that other animals can't eat. Animals that lay many eggs or poisonous ones don't usually do anything to protect them. Other parents lay fewer or tastier eggs, but they have found ways to give them a better chance to hatch. Some animals lay soft eggs in hard cases, which give protection from enemies, disease, and bad weather.

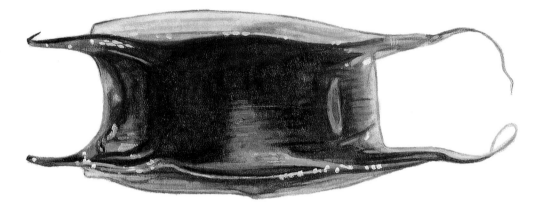

You may have found empty skate fish egg cases on the beach. These "mermaid's purses" are hard with pointed hollow horns on either end. The horns anchor the cases to seaweed, logs, and other objects in the ocean.

The praying mantis makes a soft, sticky material and whips it into an egg case. The case becomes stiff and nearly waterproof when it dries. It will hang from a twig or a stem throughout the winter, keeping out the wet weather and egg-eating birds.

Many animals bury their eggs in the ground, then leave them. All turtles, some spiders, and most lizards do. Some insects bury their eggs in burrows.

The dung beetle makes a ball of animal droppings, then digs a short tunnel. She puts the ball inside, lays a single egg on it, and seals the tunnel. After the baby beetle hatches, it will eat the dung.

A female earwig digs a short burrow and, depending on what type of earwig she is, lays twenty to fifty eggs. Most insects do not take care of their eggs. But the earwig mother does. For several weeks she cleans and turns the eggs so they won't become diseased. She guards them against predators and even stays with the babies for one to two weeks after they hatch.

Some fish bury their eggs in sand or gravel. A female brown trout digs a hole in the gravel bed of a fast-moving stream and lays her eggs there. The water current covers them with more gravel, hiding them from predators.

A number of snakes hide theirs under dead leaves or in rotting logs.

Unlike other snakes, the huge python stays with her eggs after she lays them. She basks in the sun, then curls around to incubate—or warm—them. She will also shiver. Shivering brings more heat to the eggs.

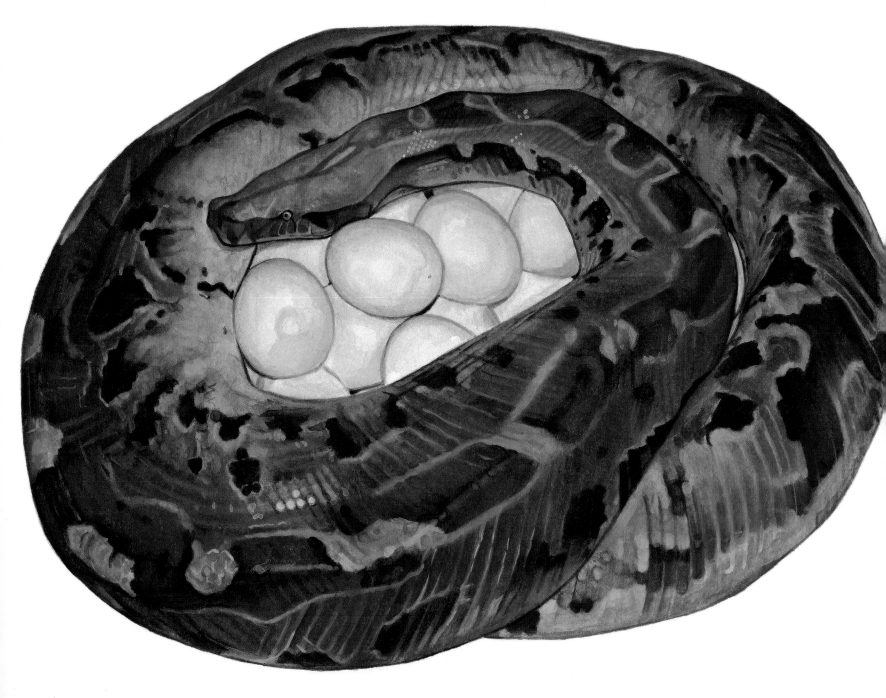

Other animals guard their eggs by brooding them in or on themselves.

The male sea horse is a fish that carries the female's eggs in a pouch on his belly.

The female spiny anteater, or echidna, is a mammal that carries her eggs in a pouch, too.

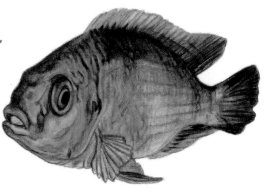

Several types of cichlids brood their eggs in their mouths. Among some cichlids, it's the father fish that takes care of the eggs. Among others, it's the mother.

Male midwife toads carry fertilized eggs attached to strings wrapped around their legs.

Female Surinam toads bear theirs in spongy holes on their backs.

The Darwin's frog broods its eggs inside the vocal sacs in its throat.

Many types of cockroaches tote their eggs in a tough protective case on the end of their abdomens.

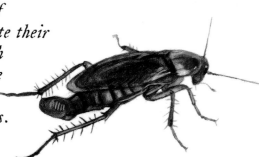

A wolf spider carries its eggs in a silken sac on its spinnerets— the fingerlike organs on a spider's rear end that help it spin silk.

Carrying eggs protects them, but it's a lot of work. Many animals protect theirs in nests instead. A male stickleback makes a mound of weeds on a pit at the bottom of a pond. He digs a tunnel through the middle and coaxes four or five female fish to lay eggs there. Another male fish, the betta, makes a nest of bubbles. Then he gathers the female's eggs and spits them into the nest.

A female alligator makes a mound of weeds, leaves, twigs, branches, and mud. She digs a pit in the center and lays fifteen to eighty eggs in it. She covers them with rotting plants, which give off heat like an oven to incubate the eggs. After about two months, the alligator tears the cover off her oven nest. The babies chip out of the shells.

Wasps and bees are famous for their nests.

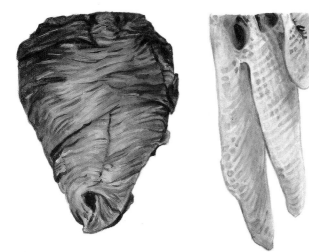

A queen honeybee will not lay an egg unless there is an empty cell. Worker honeybees decide how many eggs their queen will lay by adding or removing cells.

Yellow jackets and other wasps create nests out of paper. Honeybees build hives out of wax.

Both paper nests and hives are made up of rows and rows of cells to hold many eggs, one in each cell, all laid by the queen wasp or bee.

Potter wasps make small pot-shaped nests of mud. Each holds one egg.

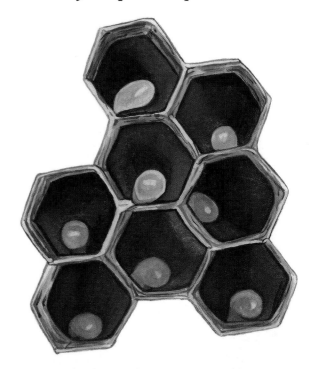

The best-known nest builders of all are birds. They make nests in and out of almost anything you can think of. The builder may be the mother, the father, or both. The same is true when it comes to incubating the eggs. Among half of all bird species, both parents take turns sitting on the nest.

Common waxbill parents sometimes incubate together, sitting side by side on their eggs in their dome-shaped nest.

The female red-legged partridge builds two nests and lays eggs in each. She incubates one clutch. The male incubates the other.

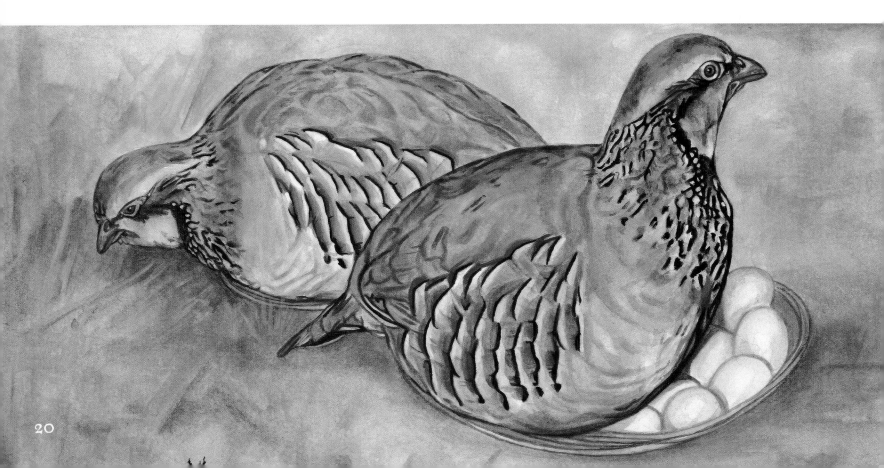

Not all birds build fancy nests—or any nests at all. Some incubate eggs on bare ground or rock ledges. Others nest inside tree holes or burrows.

Certain cuckoos lay their eggs in the nests of other birds and let the foster parents raise their young. They may even destroy the eggs of the foster parents.

The male emperor penguin incubates a single egg on his feet, covering it with a belly flap of feathered skin.

But many birds are truly remarkable builders.

Orioles use straw and bark to weave socklike nests that dangle from branches, sometimes over water.

The tailorbird of Asia sews up its fluffy nest in a leaf. It uses its beak as a needle and plant fiber as thread.

Grebes create floating nests of rotting weeds in ponds and lakes and tie them to reeds or young trees.

The job of most bird parents is not only to protect and incubate their eggs, but also to turn them. Turning eggs warms them evenly and prevents the shells from sticking to the embryos. However, few birds help their young leave their eggs. They let the youngsters hatch by themselves.

The Asian cave swiftlet has one of the most unusual nests of all. It doesn't have to find leaves, carry twigs, or build a mound. It spends thirty to forty days making a nest of its own hardened saliva high on the walls of deep caves. In this nest, the swiftlet lays two eggs. Few predators can reach these eggs. But people can. They climb ropes and ladders and gather the nests to make a soup that they consider healthful.

The time it takes for eggs to *hatch* is different for each species. Some, such as those of the tuatara, an ancient reptile, take more than a year. Others hatch in a few months or a few days.

Midboreal mayfly nymphs hatch from eggs just minutes after the mother insect drops the eggs into a stream.

Most insects use their jaws to bite their way out of their eggs, then eat what's left of them. But some have developed unusual ways of hatching.

The red admiral caterpillar swallows air until it swells and bursts the egg.

Fish and amphibians nibble through or melt their eggs to hatch. Reptiles, most birds, and mammals have an *egg tooth*—a small tooth on the top of their beak or snouts. They use it to crack or tear their shells. Then they push out. In a few days, the egg tooth falls off.

egg tooth

egg tooth

baby alligators

egg tooth

a chick

Birds hatch in a different way from reptiles or mammals.

1. *Inside its egg, a chick lies curled up.*

2. *A few days before it is ready to hatch, the chick turns, tucks its head under its right wing, and faces the round end of the egg.*

3. *A muscle in its neck begins to twitch. The chick is so large it has used up most of the space and the air inside the egg. The lack of oxygen makes the chick's neck twitch harder until the chick begins to pound the shell with its egg tooth.*

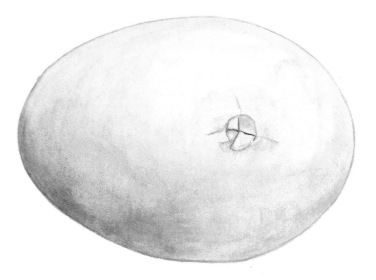

4. *Soon it makes the first crack in the shell. This is called* pipping, *and it's hard work.*

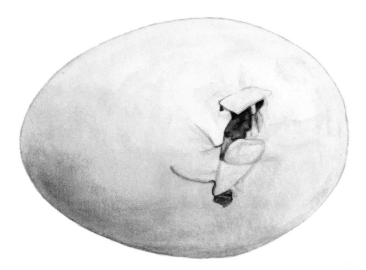

5. *After pipping, the chick rests for a few hours or even days before it finishes hatching.*

6. *Then it makes a circle or part of a circle of holes around the egg.*

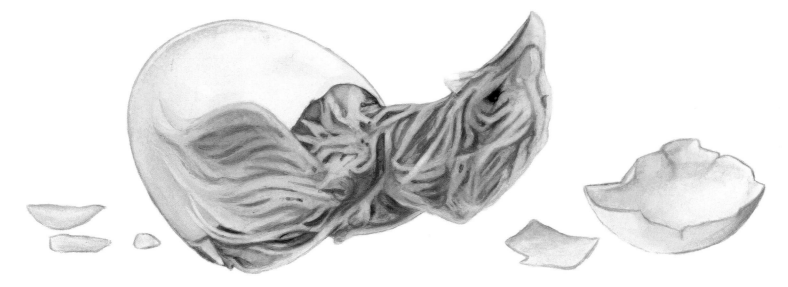

7. *The chick pushes the top off the shell and kicks out of it with its strong feet. This last stage of hatching takes less than an hour.*

When the chick is at last free of the egg, its parents will get rid of the shell. A few bird parents will eat it. But most will carry the shell away so that predators aren't alerted to newborn chicks. Some chicks will live in the nest and be fed by their parents until they are ready to fly. Others will be running or swimming, finding food for themselves within a day.

Does the swiftlet, eagle, python, platypus, bullfrog, trout, mosquito, or mantis remember the crib, boat, pond, or room it just left? Who can say? What we do know is that if each survives the adventures it will soon face, each will lay or fertilize its own eggs and bring new life into this rich, surprising world.

PROTECTING EGGS

Animals and their eggs have always faced many dangers from disease, weather, disasters, and predators. Today there are even more dangers. Most of them are caused by animals' number one enemy: people. We don't always know we're harming eggs. We need land for homes, farms, and ranches. We want oil to run our cars and heat our homes and wood to build houses and furniture. We destroy animals' habitats to get this land and these products. When animals lose space, they lay fewer eggs. Fewer eggs mean fewer babies—and fewer adults. So some animals are disappearing.

Animals and their eggs are also harmed by pollution from cars, factories, and power plants, and by the chemicals we use. The pesticides farmers and gardeners sprinkle and spray on plants can kill helpful animals as well as pests. Pesticides and fertilizers can also get into rivers, lakes, ponds, and streams. There they may kill fish, frog, and insect eggs. Waste from cattle and other farm animals also pollutes our waters and destroys eggs.

We also hurt eggs by overharvesting. Sturgeons are in danger because people have killed too many for their tasty caviar. Cave swiftlets are in trouble because some people who gather their nests for soup also remove the eggs and even the chicks.

But people can be friends instead of enemies to animals and their eggs. Nest hunters can wait to gather nests until the chicks have hatched and flown away. Fishers can raise sturgeons in fish farms to make sure new sturgeons are always being born. Gardeners and farmers can use fewer and less harmful pesticides and fertilizers and make sure these don't run into our waters. All of us can plant trees, bushes, and flowers to attract egg-laying animals. We can work to keep our environment clean and to protect parks and preserves where animals live and breed. When we visit these refuges, we can take care not to disturb the birds, turtles, and other animals nesting there.

Most of all, we can learn about the creatures around us. We can understand how much we share: we all come from eggs and we all belong on this earth. Together.

GLOSSARY

albumen: egg white. Albumen surrounds the yolk and helps protect an embryo.

amphibian: an animal with a backbone and skin that begins life in water as a larva with fishlike gills. Most amphibians develop the ability to breathe air and live on land, but some live their whole lives in water. They have smooth, moist skin (frogs and salamanders) or bumpy, drier skin (some toads), but no scales. Most amphibians lay eggs.

brood patch: an area of bare skin on a bird's belly that brings extra heat to the incubating eggs.

camouflage: the color, pattern, or shape of an egg or an animal that lets it blend into its surroundings. Camouflage disguises an egg or an animal so that predators cannot easily see it.

clutch: a single group of eggs laid by one animal.

colony: a group of the same kind of animals living together.

egg tooth: a small tooth on top of the beak or snout of a baby bird, reptile, or mammal. The egg tooth is used for chipping or tearing out of the eggshell. It falls off shortly after the baby hatches.

embryo: an unborn, developing animal.

fertilize: to join a sperm cell to an egg so that it will become an embryo.

hatch: to come out of an egg.

incubate: to keep eggs warm so they will hatch. Most birds incubate their eggs by sitting on them.

larva: a baby animal that looks completely different from its adult form, such as a tadpole or caterpillar. *Larvae* are more than one larva.

mammal: an animal with a backbone that has hair and nurses its young with milk. Mammals also breathe through their lungs and are *warm-blooded*—they have a constant body temperature no matter what the air temperature is. Only two mammals lay eggs: platypuses and echidnas.

pipping: breaking through a bird's eggshell. The first crack is called a pip.

predator: an animal that eats other animals.

reptile: an animal with a backbone that usually has scaly skin. Reptiles may live on land or in water, but they lay their eggs on land and breathe air as soon as they are born. Reptiles and amphibians are *cold-blooded*—their body temperature changes with the air temperature. Snakes, lizards, alligators, and turtles are reptiles. Most reptiles lay eggs.

roe: fish eggs.

spawn: to produce eggs (females) and shed sperm on them (males). Fish and other water animals reproduce by spawning.

sperm: a tiny cell from a male animal that joins with a female's egg to make an embryo.

yolk: the yellow part of an egg that gives the growing embryo food and water.

SOURCE NOTES

When I write a book about animals, I use a multitude of sources to find the most important and interesting information and to double-check facts. I search the Internet to find close-ups of flying fish eggs, nest box cameras that show bluebirds hatching, reptile egg incubation tables, articles on American lobsters, and a wealth of other material. For some of the Web sites I consulted, please see the list of conservation groups and organizations on p. 31.

Via e-mail and telephone, I contact biologists and zoologists (listed in the acknowledgments) in the field and at zoos, aquariums, museums, and universities. Most of all, I read articles and books. Here are some of the ones I found especially useful in writing this book.

Brooke, Michael, and Tim Birkhead, eds. *The Cambridge Encyclopedia of Ornithology*. Cambridge, England: Cambridge University Press, 1991.

Buchsbaum, Ralph. *Animals Without Backbones: An Introduction to Invertebrates.* Chicago: The University of Chicago Press, 1987.

Burton, Robert. *Bird Behavior*. New York: Alfred A. Knopf, 1985.

——. *Egg: A Photographic Story of Hatching*. New York: Dorling Kindersley, 1994.

——. *Eggs: Nature's Perfect Package*. New York: Facts on File Publications, 1987.

Ernst, Carl H., and George R. Zug. *Snakes in Question: The Smithsonian Answer Book.* Washington, D.C.: Smithsonian Institution Press, 1996.

Halliday, Dr. Tim, and Dr. Kraig Adler, eds. *The Encyclopedia of Reptiles and Amphibians.* New York: Facts on File Publications, 1998.

Lehrer, John. *The World of Turtles and Tortoises.* Blacksburg, VA: Tetra Press, 1993.

Mattison, Chris. *Encyclopedia of North American Reptiles and Amphibians: An Essential Guide to Reptiles and Amphibians of North America*. San Francisco: Thunder Bay Press, 2005.

——. *Frogs & Toads of the World*. New York: Facts on File Publications, 1987.

O'Toole, Christopher. *Alien Empire: An Exploration of the Lives of Insects*. New York: HarperCollins, Inc., 1998.

O'Toole, Christopher, ed. *The Encyclopedia of Insects*. Abingdon, England: Andromeda Oxford Ltd., 1995.

Paxton, Dr. John R., and Dr. William N. Eschmeyer, eds. *Encyclopedia of Fishes*. Sydney, Australia: Weldon Owen Pty Limited, 1998.

Perrins, Dr. Christopher M., and Dr. Alex L. A. Middleton, eds. *The Encyclopedia of Birds*. New York: Facts on File Publications, 1998.

Preston-Mafhem, Rod, and Ken Preston-Mafhem. *Encyclopedia of Insects and Spiders: An Essential Guide to Insects and Spiders of North America and the World.* San Diego: Thunder Bay Press, 2005.

Stivens, Dal. *The Incredible Egg: A Billion Year Journey*. New York: Weybright and Talley, 1974.

Stokes, Donald. *A Guide to Observing Insect Lives.* Boston: Little, Brown and Company, 1983.

Tyning, Thomas F. *A Guide to Amphibians and Reptiles*. Boston: Little, Brown and Company, 1990.

Vergoth, Karin and Christopher Lampton. *Endangered Species*. Danbury, CT: Franklin Watts, 1999.

Walters, Michael. *Birds' Eggs*. New York: Dorling Kindersley, 1994.

ACKNOWLEDGMENTS

Many thanks to Steve Aronson, Dave Hansen, Barry Koffler, Kerri McCoy, and Dorothy Hinshaw Patent; to herpetologist David Dickey, ornithologist Jackie Weicker, and entomologists Eric Quinter and Louis Sorkin, all presently or formerly of the American Museum of Natural History, and ichthyologist Paul Sieswerda of the New York Aquarium; and to my editor, Mary Cash, and the folks at Holiday House.

ORGANIZATIONS

There are many good organizations that work to protect and educate about wildlife. Here are just a few of them. You can call or write to them for information or explore their Web sites. Their sites often have links to other worthwhile organizations and to other sites just for kids.

American Museum of Natural History
Central Park West at 79th Street
New York, NY 10024
212-769-5100
http://www.amnh. org

Cornell Lab of Ornithology
http://birds.cornell.edu
For the NestBox Cam, go directly to:
http://birds.cornell.
     edu/birdhouse/nestboxcam

Defenders of Wildlife
http://www.defenders.org

Greenpeace, U.S.A.
http://www.greenpeaceusa.org

The Marine Fish Conservation Network
http://www.conservefish.org

Monterey Bay Aquarium
886 Cannery Row
Monterey, CA 93940-1085
831-648-4800
http://www.mbayaq.org

National Audubon Society
http://www.audubon.org

The Nature Conservancy
http://www.tnc.org

North American Butterfly Association
http://www.naba.org

San Diego Zoological Society
2920 Zoo Drive
San Diego, CA 92112
619-557-3969 (zoo)
760-738-5057 (park)
http://www.sandiegozoo.org

Sierra Club
http://www.sierraclub.org

Wildlife Conservation Society (Bronx Zoo)
2300 Southern Boulevard
Bronx, NY 10460
718-220-5111
http://www.wcs.org

World Wildlife Fund
http://www.worldwildlife.org

The Xerces Society
http://www.xerces.org

INDEX